The boy who bit Picasso

The boy Who bit Picasso

Antony PenRose

 Thames & Hudson

My name is **Tony**.

When I was a little boy, living on a farm in Sussex
in England, I had the most extraordinary friend.
He had deep black eyes, a big wide smile, and
absolutely amazing hands. His hands were absolutely
amazing because he could make **paintings** and
drawings and **sculptures** and collAgEs and
pots **and** PLATES and much much more.

My friend's name was

Pablo Picasso

and he was one of the

greatest

artists

who ever lived.

Picasso

When Picasso first met my mother, he thought she was so *beautiful* he painted her picture. My friends were very rude about the painting. They thought she looked so ugly she was scary! But actually it was a very good painting.

I discovered that if I took a PHOTO of my mother and drew around her face, my drawing fitted Picasso's painting exactly — except for her chin. That's because in Picasso's picture she has a huge toothy grin.

I lived with Mum and Dad at Farley Farm in Chiddingly.

Picasso was from Spain, but he lived in France.
One day he came all the way from France to visit
my family and me in England.

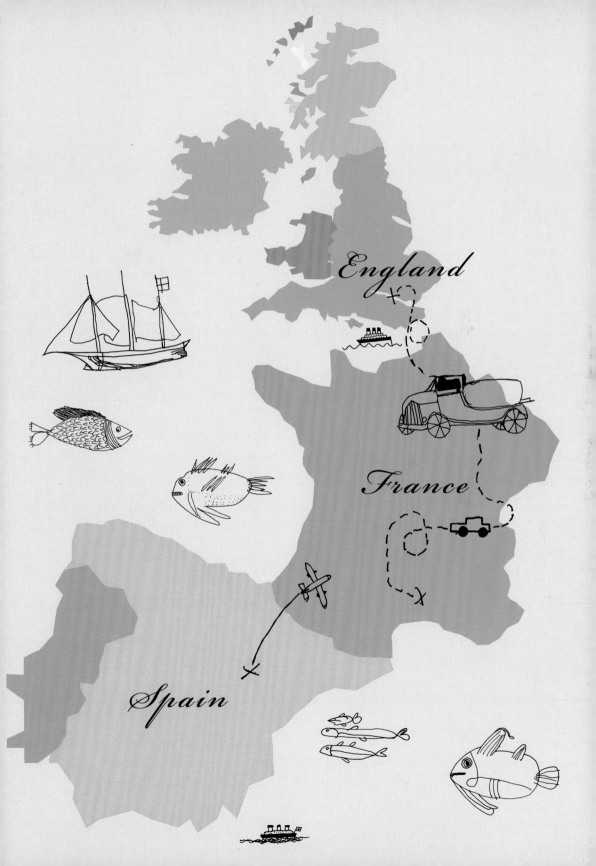

England

France

Spain

Mum was a PHOTOGRAPHER.

She took most of the photos in this book.

Dad was an **ARTIST**. When Picasso arrived at
our farm, the first thing he wanted to see was Dad's
studio. The studio was in an old building. It had a big
wooden easel to rest **paintings** on.

Picasso liked my dad's studio, but he *really* loved
animals. Straight away he said he wanted to see the
cows and meet our Ayrshire bull....

Our bull's name was William.

He was very big but friendly, and he got along really well with Picasso. He liked it when Picasso scratched his ears and talked to him in French.

That evening Picasso sat by the fire and drew William and two of his friends dressed up as flying grasshoppers!

1.11.62.
IV

My teddy bear also liked Picasso.

I couldn't speak French or Spanish, but it didn't matter at all because we didn't need a language for our games. Picasso was great fun to play with. He liked to romp around on the floor and have pretend bullfights. His tweed jacket was nice and scratchy. He smelled good, too. He smelled of cologne and French tobacco.

I don't remember this, but
Mum told everyone that one
day, when we were playing,
I got over-excited and
I naughtily bit Picasso.

Picasso turned around and
bit me right back – hard!

Just before I started to yell,
Mum heard Picasso say, in
French, 'Gosh! That's the first
Englishman I've ever bitten!'

We had a lot of fun with Picasso on our farm, but eventually it was time for him to go home to France, where he had four children of his own.

The oldest was a boy called **Paulo**.

The next oldest was a girl called **Maya**.

The next next oldest was a boy called **Claude** (he was the same age as me).

The youngest was a little girl called **Paloma**.

Claude (hiding) and Paloma

Picasso loved to draw and **paint** his children as they played while their mother watched.

Claude and Paloma's mother was called Françoise Gilot. She was very kind and gave us *delicious* chocolate treats to eat when we went to visit.

Picasso painted this **picture** of Maya and her doll.

Some of his **sculptures** look as if he made them as toys.

Françoise was also a good **ARTIST** and liked to draw her family.

Not long after Picasso had been to our farm,
I heard that my dad was going to visit him in
France, so I gave Dad my little toy London bus
as a present for Claude.

When my dad came back, he brought me a
present from Claude. It was a LITTLE WOMAN
that Picasso had made out of a TINY piece of
wood. I loved her and I put her in charge of
my Noah's Ark to take care of all the animals.

One day we all went to the south of France to visit
Picasso. His house wasn't very big, so he used an old
perfume factory nearby as a *studio*. I wish I could
remember if it still smelled of perfume. Picasso made
lots of things in his studio, including a life-sized metal
lady, which he showed me. He gave her a pretty hat
and stuck on a pair of funny eyes.

An old friend of Picasso's also came to visit. His name was Georges Braque, and he was a famous artist, too. Picasso gave Braque some doves he had made out of **pottery**.

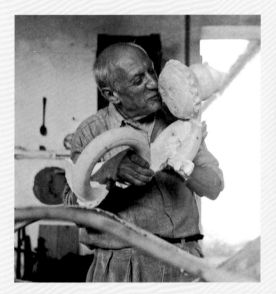

Picasso did not often use precious materials like gold or silver. Instead he used the things he found around him – things you might see in your garden or kitchen at home. He made this baby out of bits of broken pots.

He liked the pottery baby so much he made her a **mother** and a buggy as well. You can see them today in the Picasso museum in Paris.

Picasso also made this **sculpture** of a little girl skipping.
Look at her feet. Doesn't she look as if she's wearing
her mother's shoes?

At one time Picasso had a pet monkey. I never met the monkey … but I did see the sculpture Picasso made of a monkey mother with her baby.

Take a look at the mother's face. Can you see what Picasso used to make it? He used Claude's toy car.

Eventually Picasso's house became too small, so he moved to a bigger one in a nearby town. He filled his new house with strange musical instruments, African masks, birds in cages, magazines and maps, bits of junk and of course lots of things he had made.

'Has Picasso just moved in?' I asked my mother, when we went to visit.

'No,' she replied. 'He's been here quite a long time. Why do you ask?'

'Well, he hasn't put his things away,' I said.

'That's how he likes it,' she said with a laugh.

Picasso loved having fun and he let us children play with things, but he got very cross with adults if they touched anything.

However, as much as Picasso loved having fun, he also worked and worked and worked.

He was always

experimenting,

always inventing,

always making things.

Picasso kept lots of his sculptures in his house and garden. He made them from *junk*, which he transformed into **ART**. Can you see the nanny goat in the photo below? Picasso used an old basket to make her tummy, and a palm-tree branch to make her backbone. The nanny goat looked so alive I thought she was Esmeralda's mother....

Esmeralda was Picasso's pet goat. Here she is, talking to my nanny, Patsy.

Esmeralda slept in a crate outside Picasso's bedroom door. I thought this was great. At home I was never allowed to bring the farm animals inside the house.

Picasso also kept doves. He built nesting boxes for them around his bedroom windows. He used to leave the windows open so they could fly into the room and peck at seed he left on the floor. They pooed all over the floor and sometimes on the bed, but he didn't mind at all!

Here is a **picture** Picasso painted of the sunny bay of Cannes, seen from his bedroom window. Can you see some doves sitting quietly in their nesting boxes?

It wasn't always quiet in Picasso's house, though. In fact it was often like a carnival. Picasso loved disguises. Can you see which bits of his face are false?

He kept a side-table piled high with masks and funny hats. We all had to choose a disguise and wear it for most of the day. Can you see me here?

Even Mum used to dress up. She must have liked her new nose because she took this PHOTO of herself in the mirror...

Meanwhile, Picasso became more and more famous, like a rock star or football player today. But people began to bother him too much, so he moved to another house that was more private.

One time my dad visited Picasso by himself, and
that's when something special happened. Picasso
asked after me, and my dad explained that I was
unhappy because I had been sent to a very strict
school to make sure I passed my exams. Picasso
thought this was a terrible idea!

To cheer me up he sent me a little drawing. It showed a bull watching a dancer playing a flute, with a centaur listening. The drawing has cheered me up ever since.

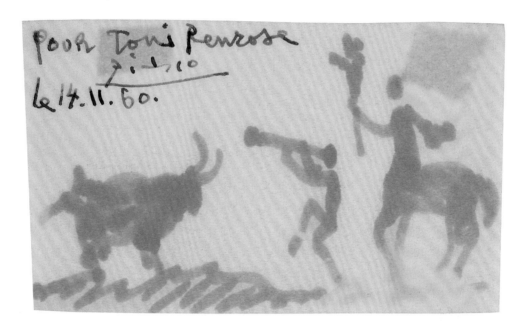

Picasso carried on creating art for many many years. When he eventually died at the ripe old age of 91, he left behind him nearly **2,000** paintings, more than **7,000** drawings, well over **1,000** sculptures and much much more. Today he is one of the most famous artists in the world … but to me he will always be my most extraordinary friend, and I hope he is now yours, too.

Picture Credits

Corgi® **p. 24 above** Picture provided by Corgi® registered trademark of Hornby Hobbies Ltd.

Françoise Gilot **p. 23 right** *The Family Walking*, 1952 (Françoise Gilot Archives G1118). © Françoise Gilot 2010.

Lee Miller **p. 2** Antony Penrose and Odette Himmuel, Farley Farm House, East Sussex, England, 1949 (original untinted); **p. 4** Antony Penrose gardening, Farley Farm House, East Sussex, England, c. 1952; **p. 7** Picasso, Villa La Californie, Cannes, France, 1957; **p. 9 right** Self-portrait, New York Studio, New York, USA, 1932 (with outline added); **p. 10** Picasso by signpost, Chiddingly, East Sussex, England, 1950; **p. 13 above** Roland Penrose and Picasso, Farley Farm House, East Sussex, England, 1950; **p. 14** Picasso, Antony Penrose and William the bull, Farley Farm House, East Sussex, England, 1950; **p. 17** Picasso and Antony Penrose, Farley Farm House, East Sussex, England, 1950; **p. 20** Claude and Paloma Picasso with Picasso ceramic, Vallauris, France, 1953; **p. 21 below** Claude Picasso and Françoise Gilot, Vallauris, France, 1949; **p. 26** Picasso and Antony Penrose beside *Woman with a Key (The Madame)*, Vallauris, France, 1954; **p. 27** Antony Penrose and Picasso, Vallauris, France, 1954; **pp. 28–29** Picasso and Georges Braque, Vallauris, France, 1954; **p. 30 left and right** Picasso making sculpture, Vallauris, France, 1954; **p. 32** Picasso and sculpture, Vallauris, France, 1954; **p. 34** Antony Penrose with Picasso's parrot, Notre Dame de Vie, France, 1962; **p. 35** Picasso's studio, Villa La Californie, Cannes, France, 1957; **pp. 36–37** Picasso playing his African xylophone, Villa La Californie, Cannes, France, 1957; **p. 38** Château de Vauvenargues, France, c. 1960; **p. 39 above** Patsy Murray and Esmeralda, Villa La Californie, Cannes, France, 1956; **p. 42** Picasso in mask, Villa La Californie, Cannes, France, 1957; **p. 43** Antony Penrose in mask with Picasso, Villa La Californie, Cannes, France, 1956; **p. 44** Self-portrait with mask, Villa La Californie, Cannes, France, 1956; **p. 46** Picasso and Roland Penrose, Villa La Californie, Cannes, France, 1956. © Lee Miller Archives, England 2010. All rights reserved.

Antony Penrose **p. 24 below, pp. 24–25** Photographs © Antony Penrose, England 2010. All rights reserved.

Roland Penrose **p. 12** Picasso, Lee Miller and Antony Penrose with friend, Farley Farm House, East Sussex, England, 1950 (original untinted); **p. 33 above** Picasso with a monkey, Antibes, France, 1939. © Roland Penrose Estate, England 2010. All rights reserved.

Pablo Picasso **p. 1** *Head of a Faun*, 1948; **p. 5** *Black Face*, 1948; **p. 8, p. 9 left** *Portrait of Lee Miller à l'Arlesienne*, 1937 (and detail, with outline added); **p. 13 below** *Two Young Bulls*, 1945; **p. 15** *Grasshopper Bulls*, design from the visitors' book of the Institute of Contemporary Arts, London, 1950; **p. 16** *Horse*, 1962; **p. 21 above** *Françoise Gilot with Paloma and Claude*, 1951; **p. 22** *Maya with a Doll*, 1938; **p. 23 left** *Woman Carrying a Child*, 1953; **p. 24 below** *'Mrs Noah'*, c. 1952; **p. 29** *Dove*, 1953; **p. 31** *Woman with Baby Carriage*, 1950; **p. 33 below** *Baboon and Young*, 1951; **p. 39 below** *Goat's Head in Profile*, 1952; **p. 40** *Dove*, date unknown; **p. 41** *The Pigeons, Cannes*, 1957; **p. 45** *Young Wood Owl*, 1952; **p. 47** *Bull, Centaur and Dancing Figure Playing Pipes*, 1960. © Succession Picasso/DACS 2010.

Saskia Praill (aged 11) **p. 18**

Katya Sanigar (aged 6½) **p. 1, p. 3** hand-lettering

Luke Veevers (aged 11) **p. 6, p. 11, p. 19, p. 48**

For Kahina and Tarik
with my love
A. P.

My beloved horse, Gypsy

The author would like to thank Ami Bouhassane, Carole Callow, Paul Davis, Lance Downie, Victoria Fenton, Laura Green, Kate Henderson, Gabi Hergert, Tracy Leeming, Brenda Longley, Kerry Negahban and Stephanie Wooller, all at Farley Farm House (www.farleyfarmhouse.co.uk).

First published in the United Kingdom in 2010 by Thames & Hudson Ltd, 181A High Holborn, London WC1V 7QX

Reprinted 2015

British Library Cataloguing-in-Publication Data
A catalogue record for this book is available from the British Library

ISBN 978-0-500-23873-8

Printed and bound in China by C&C Offset Printing Co. Ltd

To find out about all our publications, please visit **www.thamesandhudson.com**. There you can subscribe to our e-newsletter, browse or download our current catalogue, and buy any titles that are in print.